An Irish Lad

A Collection of Original and Traditional Poems, Songs and Ballads

By

William Robertson-MacDonald

Published by Pippa Publishing, PO Box 605, Taunton,
Somerset TA1 2WD, United Kingdom © 2001

ISBN 1-904171-00-1

Printed by Jensen Press, Yeovil, Somerset.

An Irish Lad

By

William Robertson MacDonald

Edited By

Wendy Every, Philippa MacDonald & Jane Hawkins

Contents

Authors' Note

This book is written, not for the pleasure of its readers but for the pleasure of its writers, in the hope that enough people will like it, and consequently buy it, to pay for the cost of publication and leave a little over ~~to spare~~ for beer and skittles and various other little luxuries in which the authors like to indulge.

Foreword.

Some people would have you believe that there is poetry in nature, some, that there is poetry in machines or in motion. They are all wrong. You will not find poetry in the sea, or in the moon, or the stars, but only in yourselves. Nor do you have to write verse to be a poet. Poetry is a way of thinking, and a way of seeing, and a way of living. It is something that flavours all your impressions and pervades all your actions — it is the philosophers stone, for it can change the most and tenderness of human circumstances into the purest gold.

Authors' Note

This book is written not for the pleasures of its readers but for the pleasure of its writers, in the hope that enough people will like it and consequently buy it, to pay for the cost of publication and leave a little over for beer and skittles and various other little lunacies in which the authors like to indulge.

Foreword

Some people would have you believe there is a poetry in nature, some, that there is poetry in machines or in motion. They are all wrong. You will not find poetry in the sea, or in the moon, or the stars, but only in yourselves. Nor do you have to write verses to be a poet. Poetry is a way of thinking, and a way of seeing, and a way of living. It is something that flavours all your impressions and pervades all of your actions – it is the philosopher's stone, for it can change the tinsel and tawdriness of human circumstances into the purest gold.

William Robertson MacDonald   c.1949

'Liam MacDonald was my father. On his death I inherited from him four small hand-written note books which I at first thought to be just traditional poems and ballads. It was a great surprise and joy to find that indeed many were his own original works. I knew him to be a good painter and modeller and had always known him to be good with words but I never knew or imagined that he had written anything more than the odd limerick for someone's birthday card.

Unlike many people who have the good fortune to be born and brought up in one place which they call 'home', my sisters and I have had something of a nomadic existence in common with many other 'forces' families. This has meant that production of this book has, for me, been a great adventure, to travel the 'happy highway where he went' as a young man. To take photographs from the exact spot that he did some 50 years before is a moving experience.

My father was a perfectionist with a sharp eye for detail, therefore, where possible all photographs relate to the geographical locations mentioned in the text. In some instances this may not be the case as we believe the primary objective of the photographs is to convey the essence and feel of the text. We apologise to any and all who may pursue a more literal stand but hope you will enjoy the book anyway.

Finally, this is very much a 'work in progress' and if you should have any information, comments, points of note or simply wish to enter a general discussion about anything contained here please write to us, or visit the interactive area of our website:
http://www.pippapublishing.co.uk

Alasdair MacDonald, October 2001

The Whitepark

Saga

Contents

Early one morning, just as
the sun was rising,
I heard a maiden singing in
the valley below.

Chorus:- Oh don't deceive me
oh do not leave me,
          How could you use
a poor maiden so?

Gay is the garland, and fresh
are the roses.
I've culled from the garden
to bind on thy brow.

Chorus:- Oh don't deceive
me oh do not leave me,
          How could you use
a poor maiden so?

Think of the vows that you made to your Mary,
Remember the bower where you vowed to be true.

Chorus:- Oh don't deceive me oh do not leave me,
How could you use a poor maiden so?

This sang the maiden, her sorrow bewailing,
And sadly she sang in the valley below.

Chorus:- Oh don't deceive me oh do not Leave me,
How could you use a poor maiden so?

Early One Morning

The Shamrock From Glenore

It was on a bright and clear St. Patrick's morning
When with thoughts of home my heart was sad and sore.
Still thinking of my dear old mother's warning
As she plucked the three leafed shamrock from Glenore.

Chorus-: It's the king of all the flowers from Killarney
Sure the likes of it you never saw before.
It grows amongst the rocks of Irish grandeur;
It's the pretty three leafed shamrock from Glenore.

Now, my mother, she is getting old and feeble
As she sits outside her lonely cabin door;
But as she sits, a rigid watch she's keeping
On the pretty three leafed shamrock from Glenore.

Chorus-: It's the king of all the flowers from Killarney
Sure the likes of it you never saw before.
It grows amongst the rocks of Irish grandeur;
It's the pretty three leafed shamrock from Glenore.

I have sailed across the broad Atlantic Ocean;
I have travelled o'er the sunny southern shore:
But nothing fills my heart with such devotion
As the pretty three leafed shamrock from Glenore

Chorus-: It's the king of all the flowers from Killarney
Sure the likes of it you never saw before.
It grows amongst the rocks of Irish grandeur;
It's the pretty three leafed shamrock from Glenore.

I treasure still, this precious little token:
It's the sweetest gem that comes from Erin's store.
It's as fresh today as when its stem was broken,
That pretty three leafed shamrock from Glenore.

Chorus-: It's the king of all the flowers from Killarney
Sure the likes of it you never saw before.
It grows amongst the rocks of Irish grandeur;
It's the pretty three leafed shamrock from Glenore.

The Dacent

Irish Lad

"Oh what'll we have for the breakfast?
My dacent Irish lad?
"We'll have pasties and salt and buttermilk"
And I think it'll no' be bad."
"Oh could we do nothing better
My dacent Irish lad?
"Do ye want to have roast beef and whisky?"
Ould woman I think you're mad

"Oh when are we going to be married?
My dacent Irish lad?
"We're going to be married tomorrow,
And I think it'll no be bad."
"Oh could we do nothing better
My dacent Irish lad?
 "Do you want to be married this
evening?
Ould woman I think you're mad!"

"Oh what'll we wear at the wedding
My dacent Irish lad?
 "We'll wear the clothes we're dressed
in
And I think it'll no' be bad."
"Oh could we do nothing better
My dacent Irish lad?
Do you want silks and satins?"
Ould woman I think you're mad!"

"Oh what'll we have for the bedding?
My dacent Irish lad?
"A battle of straw in the corner."
And I think it'll no' be bad"
"Oh! Could we do nothing better
My dacent Irish lad
"Do ye want to be smothered in feathers?"
Ould woman I think you're mad!"

"And will we have any children
My dacent Irish lad?
"We'll maybe have one or two at the
most"
And I think it'll no' be bad."
"Oh! Could we do nothing better
My dacent Irish lad?
"Do ye want them round ye in
thousands?"
Ould woman I think you're mad!"

"Oh when will we have the first one?
My dacent Irish lad?
"As soon as God allows ye"
And I think it'll no' be bad."
"Oh! Could we do nothing better
My dacent Irish lad
"Do ye want to have one this minute?"
Ould woman I think you're mad!"

The Whitepark Saga Prologue

Yhani, * thy sons have gone to bloody bridge,
And climbed, dog–tired, over Donard high;
Cursing the while, each rock and stoney ridge;
Paining the ear with swear word and with sigh.
Yet, mindful of home, and feather bed,
And fire so warm to thaw each freezing toe,
Have gone again, and to Parkmore so dead.

* Yhani (Youth Hostel Association, Northern Ireland).

Knockbarragh Park, and Tannagh Lodge also.
Yet, 'tis not of these hostels that I sing &..
 • Is't Cranny falls, or Glendum?   Nay,
But sit you down and listen while I bring
To you a tale of lovely Whitepark Bay.

Who that has heard of Whitepark Bay,
 Its rocks, its sand dunes and it cart track steep,
That would not wish, its wonders to survey,
Or in the little hostel there, to sleep.
Or sitting round the fire with comrades tune,
Tell of nights, in other hostels spent,
Or hear o' the mighty deeds that others do,
Like washing oft, or sleeping in a tent.

Thus did we converse, one with another
When Christmas tide was not so far away,
And I, MacDonald, got the bother
Of booking for us all for Whitepark Bay.

THE NATIONAL TRUST

This small building was once a Youth Hostel. The Youth Hostel Association of Northern Ireland, and the Pilgrim Trust , raised funds to purchase Whitepark Bay and handed it over to the National Trust in 1939.

Vandalism has forced the closure of public facilities and the Trust regrets that, for the present, this building has to be secured against damage.

The Dear Irish Boy

My Connor, his cheeks are as ruddy as morning;
The brightest of pearls but mimic his teeth;
While nature, with ringlets his mild brow adorning
His hair, Cupid's bow strings, and roses his breath.

Smiling; beguiling; cheering; endearing;
Together, how oft o'er the mountains we strayed:
By each other delighted, and fondly united,
I've listened all day to my dear Irish boy.

No Roebuck so swift could fly over the mountains;
No veteran, bolder meet danger on scars.
He's slightly; he's sprightly, he's clear as a fountain;
His eyes twinkle love - oh, he's gone to the wars.

The war being over and he not returned,
I fear that some dark envious plot has been laid;
Or that some cruel Goddess has him captivated
And left her to mourn, his dear Irish maid.

Kitty Magee

I've kissed and courted them all
Gentle and simple, short medium and tall
But kept a merry heart free
Till it was stole unknown by Kitty Magee.
Her laughing face; her slender waist;
Her lips might tempt a saint to taste!
Oh! Sure it was small blame to me
To lose my heart to Kitty Magee.

'Twas down at Ballina fair;
Colleens and boys were tripping it there,
And I the soul of the spree
Until I set my eyes on Kitty Magee.
Her smile so sweet; her step so neat;
Hide and seek her two little feet;
Gliding along like a swan at sea,
Handsome, winsome Kitty Magee.

And now I'm dreaming all day;
Sighing from dark till dawn, and wasting away
Like a lovebird on a tree;
Pining the long night for Kitty Magee.
At dance or wake no sport I make;
Home or out, no pleasure I take;
Nothing at all do I hear or see
But makes me think of Kitty Magee.

Oh, how will I anyone face,
Kitty astone, if you don't pity my case?
'Tis tired of living I'll be
If I don't win my darling Kitty Magee.
Oh, whisper, dear, the shrove is near;
Say the word I'm longing to hear.
Promise me, soon my own you'll be,
Roguish, coaxing Kitty Magee.

Sure it's many miles I've travelled,
And and many's the sight I've seen,
But none of them I would compare
With my little Isle of green.
And the place that I do love the best
Is in my memory still;
It's a sweet little town in the County Down,
Rathfriland on the hill.

Its slopes are speckled with emerald green,
And on them wild flowers grow:
It's covered over with cottages;
Wee houses, white as the snow.
When the sun does shine, it looks so fine
It's in my memory still,
That sweet little town in the county Down,
Rathfriland on the hill.

It stands upon its Ancient height
With view both far and wide:
You can see the purple heather
On your Mourne Mountain side
You can see the tops of Belfast,
And Bessbrooks famous mill
From that sweet little town in the County Down,
Rathfriland on the hill.

You can travel from this to Kerry
And from there to Slievenamon;
You can cross the river Shannon
And come home by lovely Bann.
You may go to see Killarney's
lakes,
But, wander where you will,
You'll never find a town like
mine,
Rathfriland on the hill.

Rathfriland On The Hill

Sure if I was in
Rathfriland
I would count myself at
home.
I'd settle down in that
wee town,
And never more would
roam.
I'd call in Johnny
Jackson's
And my glass, sure he
would fill
And I'd drink a toast to
Erin's Isle
And Rathfriland on the
hill.

A Night Run

The red glow of an open firebox
Against a dead black sky;
The starry wonder of Gods' universe
As the stilly miles slip by,
The long, lonely shrill of the whistle,
The hiss of escaping steam;
The endless cadence of the wheels on the rails;
The creak of a straining beam;
The drowsy songs the night wind sings
In the wires along the right of way,
The tender warmth of the wakening sun
Caressing a newborn day.

These are the night runs' lures;
These the "grave yarder's" pay,
So give me a call at midnight
For a dreamer can't work by day!

Adsum

Where, now, is my castle in the clouds?
My rocky fortress, structure of my thought.
Where now the happy days that were, the days
that might have been? They have but come to naught.

I builded hope on hope and dream on dream.
My hopes have failed; My dreams have faded;
Friend after friend has left me, lone and desolate,
With only that sweet memory of happy days to cheer,
Of words and thoughts too deep for words,
And naught but loneliness to end the year.

From green the leaves to russet changed,
And soon were torn from parent branch
That through the spring and summer of the year had
nurtured them.
The shadows lengthened, time wore on
And time did all that time can do
Till autumn soon was gone.
But thoughts of you
Still dwelt within my mind,
And shall do evermore
Time cannot heal the sore
Caused by a heart unkind.

There is snow on the hills this morning,
Crisp snow, pure and white:
The air on the hills is sharp and clear,
And the voice of the robin is loud in my ear:
The sky is grey, but the day is bright.

And yet, I still am restless.
My mind cannot - will not be at peace
Until my soul is free.
Born of a city, the city hold no place for me:
My haven waits, amid the glens:
Not on the basalt coast where first I thought 'twould be,
Nor on that mighty rock where once, on pleasures bent,
I sought for signs of bygone ages, and romance.
And so, when time decrees that I must rest,
'Tis there, among the pleasant fields I'll lie:
I who take this life as one great jest -
I do not wish to die! And yet,
I fear not death,
For with it, I shall find peace.

I'm a decent good Irish body

I'm a decent good Irish body
And I come from the County Tyrone,
I can do with a rale glass of toddy
And my name it is Mollie Malone.

I can whistle and sing like a starling
By the youngsters I couldn't be bet.
Whisper, I'll tell you my darling,
I'm as good as they're making them yet.

I'm a decent good Irish body
And I come from the County Tyrone.
I can do with a rale glass of toddy
And my name it is Mollie Malone.

The Weaver's Daughter

It was on a charming fine summer's
weather,
When every flower brought a pleasant
scene,
When my love he came with his hat and
feather
Unto the town of sweet Noreen.
It's "Modest Nancy, oblige my fancy,
And I'll buy you a bright chain of gold."

I would not spoil my good reputation
For all the gold you have in store,
For they are but heartless that e'er
would venture
To fix their minds on gold, I'm sure.
Oh she is my fancy; her name is Nancy,
The weaver's daughter of sweet Noreen.

Part One
The Departure

But, lest I, in passing, should forget,
I'll introduce "Jake" Pringle who did grieve
When from his bed he had to get
At half past four, or five o'clock,
To meet us all at six fifteen
Inside the station, by the rock
Whereon are carved, plain to be seen,
The names of many warriors brave
Soldiers of the king and queen,
Who died by air, on land, in wave.

I reckon now 'tis time to introduce
The gallant band, who, on that ill– starred day.
Did sally past the ruins of Dunluce
And so arrive fatigued, at Whitepark Bay
And also they, (the girl and fellows twain)
Who, fearing they might miss their Christmas pie.
Came via Ballycastle, on the evening train
Arriving not until the moon was high.

Beth Dickey, first, I'll introduce to you
A maiden fair, in all the bloom of youth
With her came sister Mollie, who
I know not much about, to tell the truth
Except that she doth cast a wary eye
Upon bold Alex Johnston, who doth gaze
With seeming love on her, *and I
Shall later in this ditty sing his praise
And how he did, a blackened eye receive.

*Alex and Mollie married 11th February 1947

I now must mention Joseph Currie,
Ethel Graham and Boomer (Bill),
Who, unlike us, in are great hurry
Stayed home through the day, until
When the night her cloak had spread
Over lonely vale and hill,
Hurried to the station dead
Where, late, they mounted on the train
As we did earlier in the day

When thus we travelled to Coleraine
Where we changed but not so they,
For they did change at Ballymoney
To the branch line (narrow gauge).
(The fare is fourpence extra money,
 But Jake says, "Worth a fortnights
wage!)

Nevertheless, as I have told,
We at Coleraine did arrive
And, finding the station mighty cold,
A ceilidhe we did now contrive
Upon the platform there, to hold.
Then as mornings earliest ray
Turned the sky a paler blue;
With the dawn of Christmas Day,
The down line local came in view.

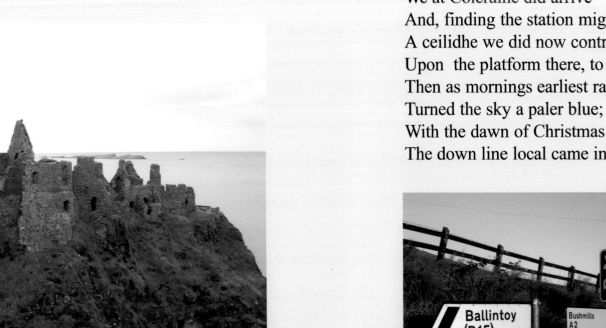

The Belfast Mountains

Upon the Belfast Mountains I heard a lovely maid
Making her lamentation down by yon crystal stream.
She says, "I am confin-ed all in the bonds of love
By a brisk young weaver who does inconstant prove."

She says, "My loving Johnny, don't treat me with disdain,
To leave me here behind you, my sorrows to be-wail."
She clapped her hands and cried, "Johnny, love, farewell,
And to those Belfast Mountains my story I will tell.

It's not your Belfast mountains can give to me relief,
Nor is it their power to ease me of my grief.
He clasped his hands around me like violets round the vine,
That bonnie weaver laddie that stole this heart of mine.

If I had all the diamonds that grow in yonder hill,
I would send them to my laddie if he would for me feel.
If I had a tongue to prattle I'd tell my love fine tales;
To my bonnie weaver laddie, my heart I would reveal.

Now since my love is gone from me, his face I'll never see;
He's left me here behind him in woe and misery.
But I hope he will return back safe to me again,
That bonnie weaver laddie that's won this heart of mine."

I've left Ballymoney a long way behind me:
To better my fortune I've crossed the salt sea,
And och! I'm alone, not a creature to mind me
My poor heart is weary, as weary can be.
I think of the buttermilk fresh from the churning,
The beautiful fields and the emerald plain;
Och, and often my thoughts in their fancy are turning
To sweet Ballymoney and Norah Macshane.

I sigh for the turf fire so cheerily glowing
When, barefoot, I trudged in from toiling all day,
And I'm wishing to God that soon I'll be going
To that bright-eyed colleen whose smile cheered my way.
In truth, I believe that I'm half broken—hearted
To my country and love I must get back again.
For I've never been happy at all since I parted
From sweet Ballymoney and Norah Macshane.

Och there's something so sweet in the land I was born in;
I sigh for the cottage; its roof made of thatch.
How pleasant the sound of the lark in the morning
What music in lifting the rusty old latch.

"Tis true I'd no money, but then I'd no sorrow
I could handle a hurl, or race through the rain.
And as sure as the sun rises brightly tomorrow,
I'll return to Ballymoney and Norah Macshane.

Norah Macshane

The Green Bushes

As I was a walking one morning in May
To hear the birds sing, and see lambkins at play,
I espied a young maiden, and sweetly sang she
Down by the green bushes where she chanced to meet me.

"Oh why are you loitering here, pretty maid?"
"I'm waiting for my true love" softly she said.
"Shall I be your true love and will you agree
to leave your own true love and follow with me?

I'll give you fine beaver and fine silken gown;
I'll give you smart petticoats, flounced to the ground;
I'll bring you fine jewels, and live just for thee
If you'll leave your own true love and follow with me".

"I want none of your jewels, or fine silk, or hose,
for I'm not so poor as to marry for clothes,
but if you will promise to be constant and true,
then I'll leave my own true love and marry with you.

Come, let us be going, kind sir, if you please.
Oh let us be going from under these trees,
For yonder is coming my true love, I see,
Down by the green bushes where he hopes to meet me."

And when he came there and found she was gone,
He looked very sheepish and cried, quite forlorn,
"She's gone with another and forsaken me
and left the green bushes where she vowed to meet me!"

The Mutton

I remember my young days for younger I've been;
I remember my young days by the Mutton Burn stream.
It's not marked on the world's map and nowhere to be seen,
That wee river in Ulster; that Mutton Burn stream.

Sure it flows under bridges, takes many a turn;
Sure it turns round the mill wheel that grinds the folk's corn,
And it wimples thro' meadows and keeps the land clean,
Belfast Lough it soon reaches, that Mutton Burn stream

Sure the ducks love to swim in it from morning till e'en:
While they dirty the water, sure they make themselves clean,
Och I've seen them a diving till their tails were scarce seen,
wadding down in the bottom of the Mutton Burn stream

Now the ladies from Carry, I oftimes have seen
Taking down their fine linen to wash in the stream,
And no powder nor soap used a wee dunk makes them clean;
It has great cleansing powers, this Mutton Burn stream.

And it cures all diseases, tho' chronic they've been;
It will rid you of fatness, or cure you of lean.
Sure the jandies itself now, weak heart or strong spleen
All give way to the powers of the Mutton Burn stream.

Once a partying at night time, when I'd not be seen:
And they aye give good parties that live round the stream.
Coming home in the morn' time. All calm and serene,
Sure I slipped and I fell in that Mutton Burn stream.

Burn Stream

I know where I'm going,
And I know who's going with
me;
I know who I love
But the dear knows who I'll
marry.

Some say he's dark;
Some say he's bonny;
But fairest of them all
Is my handsome, winsome
Johnny.

I have stockings of silk;
Shoes of fine green leather;
Combs to bind my hair;
And a ring for every finger.

Feather beds are soft
And painted rooms are bonny,
But I would leave them all
To be with my love, Johnny.

I know where I'm going
And I know who's going with me;
I know who I love,
But the dear knows who I'll marry.

I Know Where I'm Going

THE FIELDS

I've seen the spring in England,
And oh, 'tis pleasant there
When all the buds are breaking,
And all the land is fair,
But all the time, the heart of me,
The sweeter, better part of me,
Is sobbing for the Robin
In the fields of Ballyclare.

OF BALLYCLARE

I've seen the spring in England,
And oh, 'tis England's fair
With spring time in her beauty,
A queen beyond compare,
But all the time, the soul of me,
Beyond the poor control of me,
Is sighing to be flying
To the fields of Ballyclare.

I've known the spring in England
And now I know it here
This many a month I've longed for
The opening of the year,
But oh, the Irish mind of me
I hope 'tis not unkind of me
Is turning back with yearning
To the fields of Ballyclare.

Then on board the train we tumbled
And among our rucksacks jumbled
Searched for grub while Pringle grumbled,
 "The hunger is on me".
Then had we biscuit, buns and cake;
 Hamburgers that my ma did make.
And gingerale, our thirst to slake
In lieu of "Rosy Lee".
The train did not go very fast,
But soon we had thro' Portstewart passed
And into Portrush came at last,
And quit the N.C.C.*

*N.C.C. Northern Counties Committee

We ate some more from out our store
Of grub and chocolate (loose)
And on we went, tho' nearly spent,
Past gaunt and grim Dunluce.
Past Ballintrae that lovely bay,
We staggered feeling thin.
O'er many hills into Bushmills
Where we hoped to get some "din".

From Portrush town we wandered down
And hiked out by the sea
Along the Strand to White rocks grand
Where up the path strode we
Back to the road, though each one's load
Seemed heavy and heavier be;
And when a bus sped right past us
It didn't increase our glee

But on that day, to our dismay,
The cafés were all shut.
Quoth Alex bold, "when all is told,
I guess we are in a rut!"
"Upon my soul, we'll have to thole!"
 (So spoke the Nobel John)
"You're telling us!" I start to cuss,
"Well lets be getting on".

We staggered up the gray road
That lies along the hill
With six long miles behind us,
And six to cover still.
Past Dundanave Carnkirk too
(And paused there for a while)
Then on to Lisnagunogue
With a rest at every style.

Part 2
A Days Journey

My feet were sore.
I racked my brains to think of
something bright
To say. Then as we turned the bend
Templastra came in sight.
We're nearly there," I told them;
They raised a faint "hooray!"
And ere another half–hour passed
We reached sweet Whitepark Bay.

We signed the book in Dan's house
And left our cards as well.
We stumbled down the cart track,
And Beth she nearly fell.
But, anyhow we got there and
were we glad?
I'll say!
I never have been more pleased
To be in Whitepark Bay.

As winter was brawling o'er high hills and mountains,
And dark were the clouds o'er the deep rolling sea,
I spied a wee lass as the daylight was dawning;
She was asking the road to sweet Carnlough Bay.

I said, "My wee lassie, I canna well tell ye
The number of miles, or how far it might be,
But if you'll consent, I'll convoy ye a wee bit
And show ye the road to sweet Carnlough Bay.

Carnlough Bay

Ye turn to the right and go down by the church yard;
Cross over the river and down by the sea.
We'll drop in Pat Hamill's and have a wee drop there
Just to help us along to sweet Carnlough Bay."

Here's a health to Pat Hamill; likewise the wee lassie,
And to every laddie that's list'ning to me,
And ne'er turn your back on a bonnie wee lassie
When she's asking her road to sweet Carnlough Bay.

KITTY OF COLERAINE

As beautiful Kitty, one morning was tripping,
With a pitcher of milk, from the fair of Coleraine.
When she saw me, she stumbled ,the pitcher it tumbled,
And all the sweet buttermilk watered the plain.
"Oh what shall I do now? 'Twas looking at you now
Sure, such a pitcher I'll ne'er see again!"
"Twas the pride of my dairy, och Barney Macleary,
You're sent as a curse on the girls of Coleraine!"

I sat down beside her and gently did chide her
That the loss of the pitcher should cause her such pain.
A kiss then I gave her, and before I did leave her,
She vowed for such pleasure she'd break it again.
'Twas haymaking season; I can't tell the reason,
But troubles will never come single 'tis plain,
For, very soon after poor Kitty's disaster,
The divil a pitcher was whole in Coleraine!

Oh, Grandson of Domkerwell,
You talk of your northland;
Your cliffs and your White Sea,
Where thunder the breakers;
Where sea-birds go screaming
And soaring on upwind
What know you, oh North man,
What know you of Tin Owen?

In Reply

You can have your cliffs and your seabirds;
Your castles with their dungeons,
Where the cold, stark wind goes howling
And the rain does often pour.
But give to me the country
Far in the heart of Ulster,
The land that is called Tin Owen,
When I think my heart grows sore.

Have you ever climbed a small hill
 In the summer, or the autumn,
When the sun is near to setting
Far away out in the west?

Have you ever felt the stillness that
Flows o'er all the country
As the birds and beasts do homage
To the land I love the best?

Far below us twines the river,
 It is known as the Blackwater,
And there the herds of cattle
 Cool their shanks and swish the
flies.

There the willows billow gently
 As the cooling breeze of evening
Blows across this land of heaven;
Can't you hear how soft it sighs?

Far below, the sun has set now
 And the glory of the flatland
All is bathed in golden vapour
In the light we call the kype.

It's the light that makes you
wonder
 And ponder on all deep
things;
It's the light that makes you
worship,
And your tears forget to wipe.

But the darkness now is falling
And it's time that we were
moving
From this seat among the
hilltops,
For I see a mist below.

Now the night sounds are
beginning;
There's a bat below us flitting
As he dodges for his dinner
Yes, 'tis time that we should go.

But the darkness now is
falling
And it's time that we
were moving
From this seat among
the hilltops,
For I see a mist below.

Now the night sounds are
beginning;
There's a bat below us flitting
As he dodges for his dinner
Yes, 'tis time that we should go.

Part 3 Christmas Dinner

Beth and Mollie fetched the milk
And pasties for our tea;
Pringle lit the primus stove
And so it was left to me
To lay the fire and light it
While Alex chopped some wood.
Then, when we got it going strong,
We started on the food.

We had our Christmas dinner
Tho' it certainly was late
But och, the time's of no account
If you're right about the date.
We'd a feast fit for Lord Woolton
And mind, I tell no lie,
We couldn't have done better
 If we knew we were to die.

We'd soup to start, at least upon the tin
 The label said 'twas soup, so I just heaved it in.
And then, in case the flavour was not strong,
 I added several "oxo 'cubes
But maybe that was wrong?
Then we'd turkey (canned of course),
But for all I knew, it might have been horse.
Though I suppose I must admit it looked like
Turkey just a bit.

The spuds were good that's true enough;
The turnip well, twas rather tough.
Then the third course came in view a duff.
(A rather small one) true, but supplemented by a
mess
Made up by me, which, naytheless,
Tho' 'twasn't thick nor twasn't thin was soon with
Plum duff shovelled in.

'Twas then one noble friend John G.
Played his small part, and poured the tea
Then, while sitting round and drinking we
Be took ourselves to thinking, wishing
against each
Others wishes that someone else would wash
the dishes
Howanever, noble John with Alex' said, the
job got done.

Must I go bound?

Must I go bound and you go free?
Must I love the lass that wouldn't love me?
Was e'er I taught so poor a wit
As to love the lass would break my heart?

I put my finger to the bush
To pluck the finest rose,
I pricked my finger to the bone,
But ah, I left the rose behind.

So, must I go bound, and you go free?
Must I love the lass that wouldn't love me?
Was e'er I taught so poor a wit
As to love the lass would break my heart?

I've a nice slated house; I've a cow or two at grass;
I've a plant garden running by the door.
I've a shelter for the hens and a stable for the ass,
And what could a man want more?
I dunno ----- may be so,
And a bachelor is easy and he's free,
But I've lots to look after and I'm living all my
lone
And there's no one looking after me.

My father often tells me I
should go and have a try
For to get a girl that owns a
bit of land
And I know the way he says it
that there's someone in his eye
And me mother has the whole
thing planned.
I dunno ----- may be so,
And 'twould mollify them
greatly to agree,
But there's little Bridget Flynn
and its her I want to win
Though she never sets her eye
on me.

Little Bridget Flynn

Now there's a little girl that is worth her
weight in gold,
And that's a decent dowry, don't you see?
And I mean to go and ask her, as soon as I
get bold
If she'll come and have her eye to me.
I dunno -----would she go!
But I'd like to have her sitting on my knee,
And I'll sing like a thrush on a hawthorn
bush
When she comes to have her eye to me.

There's one thing between us that I do confess

That I go to meeting and my true love goes to Mass.

But for to go to Mass with him I'd count it no great toil

And the world I would wander with you Johnny Doyle.

A horse and side saddle did my father provide,

He thought to get me married to be another's bride;

A horse and side saddle did my father prepare,

With six noble footmen to wait on me there.

Johnny Doyle

We rode all along until we came to Belfast town,

Our horses being stabled and the footmen seated down.

While they were at their merriment I had my own toil

For my heart is on the ocean with you Johnny Doyle.

It was in my dear brother's arms that I was carried home;

My mother she conducted me into my own bedroom.

My own bed being softest, my head I did lay down

For to seek consoling sorrow, my body it was found.

"I'll send for Johnny Doyle for you, my own darling child;

I'll send for Johnny Doyle for you, my own heart's delight."

"You'll send for Johnny Doyle, mother, but I fear it is too late

For death you are a coming, and sad is my fate.

Now death you are coming, you are welcome to me.

From the pains of true love I'm sure you'll set me free.

There is more trouble in my mind than my poor tongue can tell

And my heart is on the ocean with you, Johnny Doyle."

Hush a ba birdie, croon, croon,
Hush a ba birdie, croon;
The sheep are gane tae the sil'er wood,
And the coos are gane tae the broom,
broom,
And its' brow milkin' the kye, kye,
And its' brow milkin' the kye;
The birds are singin; the bells are
ringin'
The red deer come a galloping bye,
bye.

Hush a ba birdie, croon,
croon,
Hush a ba birdie, croon;
Your father's gone to the mill
again,
To mak' the wheel gae' roun'
roun'
For they're busy thrashin' the
corn, corn,
For they're busy thrashing' the
corn;
We'll want a deal for the
bairnies meal,
When he wakens up in the
morn, morn.

Hush a ba birdie

Hush a ba birdie, croon, croon,
Hush a ba birdie, croon;
Your mither is weary wi'
watchin' here
And fain wad she lie down,
down,
An to rest she'll no' be blate,
blate,
An to rest she'll no' be blate;
The fire is sinkin' an' mither is
thinkin'
Her bairnies maun sleep, for it's
late, late.

Dunluce

Dunluce castle was built in the 16-17th century by the MacDonnells, a branch of the Clan MacDonald.

The castle was said to be 'a stronghold, impossible to conquer before gunpowder'.

A section of the kitchen fell into the sea one night during dinner in 1639.

There is a sea cave under the castle with direct boat access to the sea, the MacDonnells kept boats here for a quick escape should the need arise.

Not for naught were thou built, where, today,
The ruins reign, still proud, as if at bad
Against the ravages of time.   Salute to thee,
Historic guardian of our land and sea.

Despair must thou have caused within the hearts of men,
Roaming the cold, bleak, northern seas in search of
ill won-gain.
Hoping, mayhap, to find some feebly guarded their crag.
Which they might quickly take, thereon to plant their flag.

Silent now, thy cobbled banquet halls.
Where men once dined and died.   Inside your walls
Strong chieftains reigned in feudal pomp and state.
Planning and plotting that they might be great.

Their petty greatness lasted but a life,
An age of toil, of sorrow, and of strife;
But, thou has stood from time beyond recall
And tho' derelict and roofless shall not fall.

'Liam MacDonald lived at Dunluce House c1951-52 while stationed at RAF Ballykelly, the photographs show how it was then and is now.

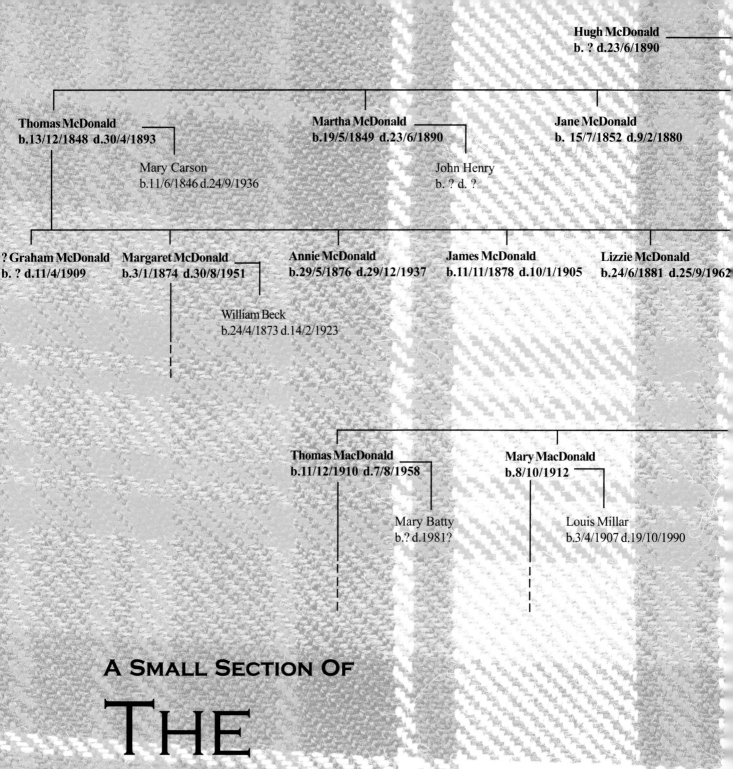

Hugh McDonald
b. ? d.23/6/1890

Thomas McDonald
b.13/12/1848 d.30/4/1893

Mary Carson
b.11/6/1846 d.24/9/1936

Martha McDonald
b.19/5/1849 d.23/6/1890

John Henry
b. ? d. ?

Jane McDonald
b. 15/7/1852 d.9/2/1880

? Graham McDonald
b. ? d.11/4/1909

Margaret McDonald
b.3/1/1874 d.30/8/1951

William Beck
b.24/4/1873 d.14/2/1923

Annie McDonald
b.29/5/1876 d.29/12/1937

James McDonald
b.11/11/1878 d.10/1/1905

Lizzie McDonald
b.24/6/1881 d.25/9/1962

Thomas MacDonald
b.11/12/1910 d.7/8/1958

Mary Batty
b.? d.1981?

Mary MacDonald
b.8/10/1912

Louis Millar
b.3/4/1907 d.19/10/1990

A SMALL SECTION OF

THE
MACDONALD
FAMILY TREE

92

Annie Gilmore
b. ? d.4/7/1891

Mary McDonald
b.13/2/1854 d.29/5/1913

Annie McDonald
b.30/8/1856 d.25/8/1879

Sarah McDonald
b.14/6/1858 d.1912?

Lizzie McDonald
b.23/4/1862 d.2/2/1926

John Hill
b.1846? d.27/11/1893

James Kane
b. ? d.?

Thomas McDonald
b.22/3/1885 d.2/1/1950

Robert McDonald
b.28/5/1888 d.18/5/1947

Samuel McDonald
b.5/12/1890 d.2/8/1966

Margaret Robertson
b.25/4/1890 d.7/4/1950

Adeline Richmond
b.13/12/1888 d.14/4/1958

Winifred Scott
b.? d.9/5/1984

William Robertson MacDonald
b.8/5/1923 d.23/7/1996

Kennethina Fraser
b.23/3/1917

93

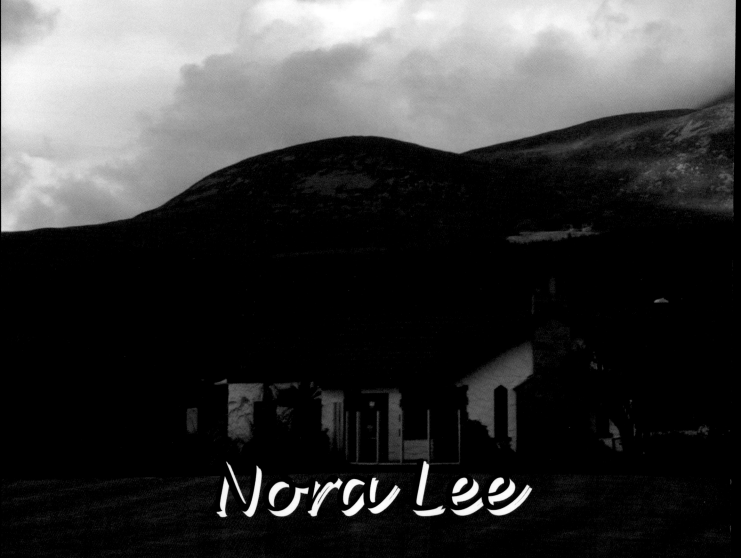

*All beside a small green
hill,*
"Neath a Rowan tree,
*Sang a blackbird sweet and
shrill,*
Sang of Nora Lee.
Nora Lee; Nora Lee;
Laughing thro the fair.
*Springtime goes the way you
walk,*
And swallows in the air.

*In your blush the rose was
born;*
In your voice a song;
*Your soft eyes, a bright blue
star*
Lost its light among.
Nora lee; Nora Lee;
Maid with golden hair.
*Springtime goes the way you
walk*
Swallows in the air.

Nora Lee

When the mistletoe is green
"Midst the winter snows.
Sunshine, in your face is seen;
In your cheeks, the rose.
Nora Lee; Nora Lee;
Though the trees be bare
Springtime goes the way you
walk;
Swallows in the air.

Though beside the small
green hill
No glad bird may sing,
In my heart your song en-
dures;
Take my golden ring.
Nora Lee; Nora Lee;
Love and life we'll share.
Springtime goes the way you
walk;
Swallows in the air.

Oh Father, Father,

It was early, early in the month of May
Down by the green fields I chanced to stray;
I heard a female sigh and say
The lad she loved was gone far away.
"Oh Father, Father, build me a boat
For it's o'er the ocean I long to float
To watch the big ships as they pass by
And to enquire of my sailor boy."

She was not long floating on the deep
When three large vessels she chanced to meet
Saying "Captain, Captain, come tell me true
Was my true love Willie on board with you?"
"What coloured clothes did your Willie wear?
What colour was your love's hair?"
"His hair was light and his eyes were blue
And he wore a coat of navy blue"

Build Me a Boat

"Oh, no, no, maiden, he is not here.
He's swamped and drowned I dreadly fear;
It was at Green Island as we passed by
We lost three more and your sailor boy."
She wrung her hands and tore her hair
Like any fair maid in deep despair;
She dashed her small boat against the rocks
Saying, "What will I do now my love is lost?"

"Now I'll sit down, and I'll write a song
And if I write it, I'll write it long;
For every line sure I'll shed a tear
And for every verse I'll cry Willie dear.
Oh dig my grave and dig it deep;
Put a marble stone at my head and feet,
And in the middle put a turtle dove
To let the world all know that I died of love."

Part 4 The Others Arrive

Having had our fill of tea, we must leave the good John G;
Alex, Mollie, Beth and me, and back to Belfast fly to see
Our intrepid comrades three; Ethel Graham and Joseph C;
(Not forgetting William B) on the puff puff charging free
Out of town and o'er the lea

Now that they ensconced are safe inside a Pullman car;
Now that they are on their way, let me tell you how, today.
Boomer yes, Bill Boomer; he who now with Joe and Ethel G.
Is on the way to Ballymoney he who thought it very funny
When at the Yhani "Get together" I asked them all to decide
Whether with me, on the morning train, they would travel to
Coleraine
Come down with Alex Beth and Moll to wish "Bon Voyage" to
Us all!

Well, after all, see what I mean?
Down at the station at six fifteen!
When anyone with brain less dead
Would snug and warm have been, in bed.
"The mans insane" said Jake to me and for once at least
I had to agree.
"Though meaning no offense to him it really is the ruddy limit!"
And when we asked him why he'd done it, calmly answered,
"Just for fun,"

In Ballymoney station, lamps are bright and shouts of porters
Echo all around. Our friends from out their carriage now alight
And get in the train for Ballycastle bound
The green flag waves; the guard his whistle blows, and once
Again they're well upon their way, but thro' the coach, a steady
Draught there blows which chills them to the bone (or so they say).

The remains of Ballycastle Narrow Gauge Railway Station

Its four short miles to Dervock, and
five more to Armoy but
The wee tank locomotive goes no
faster than a toy.
How anever "tempus fugit" even on
the narrow gauge, and soon the
Tiny loco's puffing bravely down
Glentaise
They at last reach Ballycastle where
they do not long delay,
But shouldering their rucksacks they
set out for Whitepark Bay.

About this time, in Whitepark Bay, in the hostel by the sea,
We were dozing round the fire; (Alex, Moll, Beth, Jake and me).
I looked my watch: "It's getting late," I said to honest John.
"You're right indeed", said he to me, "I'll get the kettle on."
(For we had promised faithfully upon the previous day
To have the kettle ready boiled when'er they reached the bay).

The kettle wasn't boiling long when steps were heard outside;
The door was ope'd, and in there strode the yhanis joy and pride,
Bill Boomer, closely followed by Miss Graham and Joseph C
"We're nearly dead with cold." They cried,
 "Quick, pour us out some tea".

We thawed them out with strong hot tea and fed them up with cake;
"You're very late", we told them then; says Joe, Och shut yer bake",
He said, "we've had an awful time; we've walked for hours and hours
What with the cold the dark and all, and these old 'rucks' of ours,
We're nearly foundered, sure enough, and downwards from our knees.
Our feet and legs weigh down like lead&.. ah, &I'll have some
More tea please".

At last we got them warmed again, and
sitting round the fire,
We thought, 'we're all so very tired we'd
better all retire".
And so my friends, we all turned in with
little more delay,
And that I think is quite enough about
our Christmas day

We have scenes sublime and grand
In our dear old native land
We've the beauty wild of river, rock and tree;
We have many a flowering vale
Where the zephyrs pitful gale
From the distance brings the moaning of the sea.

But wherever we may roam
Far from our dear native home,
We will think back on our early days with joy
Of the days we've spent in thee,
Lovely village by the sea,
In our well remembered native Ballintoy.

I have strayed along the shore
When the midnight billow's roar
Was re echoed back from many a fairy cave
When Rathlins flashing light
Gleamed across the billows bright
Like a shining silvery pathway o'er the wave.

Dear Port Bradden's rocky shore
And the cliffs of old Bengore
Looked like old familiar faces to my view,
Where the towering cliffs arise,
Soaring upward to the skies,
And the seaweed shines beneath the billows blue.

We have legends old and grey
Of a race long past away,
Ere the truths of Christianity were known.
Still in fancy can we see
Grim warriors bend the knee
As they kneel around Mount Druid's altar stone.

Steep isles cliffs we still recall,
Larry Bane, and Brocky tall;
And the shore we wandered often, as a boy,
Or the bridge of Corrick a rode,
Shining in the misty shade
Near the pretty little port, of Ballintoy.

Sweet Ballintoy

Twas in the town of Tralee an apprentice to trade I was bound
With a plenty of bright amusement for to see the days go round.
Till misfortune and ruin came over me which caused me to stray
from my land,
Far away from my friends and companions to follow her black
ribbon band.

Chorus: - Oh her eyes they shone like diamonds, you'd think she
was queen of the land
With her hair thrown over her shoulders tied up with
a black ribbon band.

As I went down the Broadway not intending to stay very long
I met with a ticklesome damsel as she came tripping along.
A watch she pulled out of her pocket and slipped it right into my
hand.
And the very first day that I met her, bad luck to her black rib-
bon band.

Chorus: - Oh her eyes they shone like diamonds, you'd think she
was queen of the land
With her hair thrown over her shoulders tied up with
a black ribbon band.

104

Before judge and jury next morning we both of us did appear
And a gentleman swore to the jewelry and the case against us
was clear.
For seven years transportation right into Van Diemen's land
Far away from my friends and relations to follow her black
ribbon band.

Chorus: - Oh her eyes they shone like diamonds, you'd think she
          was queen of the land
           With her hair thrown over her shoulders tied up with
          a black ribbon band.

Oh all you young Irish lads, a warning take by me;
Beware of those ticklesome Colleens that are knocking around in
Tralee.
They'll treat you to whiskey and poteen until you're not able to
stand
And before you have time to leave them you are in Van Diemen's
land

Chorus: - Oh her eyes they shone like diamonds, you'd think she
          was queen of the land
           With her hair thrown over her shoulders tied up with
          a black ribbon band.

The Black Ribbon Band

Van Diemen's Land is now known as Tasmania

Down
By The
Sally Gardens

Down by the Sally Gardens
My love and I did meet.
She passed the Sally Gardens
With little snow - white feet.
She bid me take love easy
As the leaves grew on the tree,
But I being young and foolish
With her did not agree.

In a field by the river
My love and I did stand,
And on my leaning shoulder
She placed her snow-white hand;
She bid me take life easy,
As the grass grows on the weirs,
But I was young and foolish
And now am full of tears.

Because I love you so, Machree,
There's no one else but you:
Your laughing eyes have conquered me
What'er your will, I'll do.
Like sunrise on the Wicklow hills
You set my heart aglow.
My bosom, with sweet rapture, thrills
Because I love you so.

Because I Love

Because I love you so Mavrone,
I hasten when you call.
I live for you and you alone,
I'd gladly give you all.
Like sunrise on the Wicklow hills
You set my heart aglow.
My bosom, with sweet rapture, thrills,
Because I love you so.

ou So Machree

The Big Turf Fire

Oh, the big turf fire, and the hearth swept clean,
Sure there's no one hald so happy as meself and
Paddy Keane.
To the baby in the cradle you can hear her
mammy say
"Wouldn't you hould yer whisht, alannah, till I
wet your daddy's tea."

Oh, the man that I work for is a richer man
than me,
But somehow in this world, sure we never could
agree.
He has big towering mansions and castles over
all
But sure I wouldn't change them for my
Little marble hall.

I've a nice little house and a tidy bit of land
Sure you wouldn't see a finer on the side of
Knocnacran.
I've no piano in the corner and no pictures on
the wall,
But I'm somehow quite contented in my little
marble hall.

Falling waters
Cascading thro' my
dreams
Recall to my memory
The long gaunt head of
Garron
And Glenariffs' tumbling
streams.

Crashing waters
roaring in my mind
Restore to my vision
The cold, deep sea of Moyle
Churned by the winter
wind.

Waters meeting waters
Where the green glen meets
the sea,
Ever call my thoughts to
Antrim
To the blue hills, the bright
streams,
And to thee.

Falling Waters

The Engineers Hymn

Oft when I feel the engine swerve
As o'er strange rails we fare,
I strain my eyes around the curve
For what awaits us there?
Then swift and free, she carries me
thro' yards unknown at night
I look along the line to see
That all the lamps are white

The blue light marks the crippled
can;
The yellow signals "slow";
The red light is the danger light;
The white light let her go!
Again the open fields we roam,
And, when the night is faire
I gaze up at the starry dome
And wonder what's up there.

For who can speak for those that
dwell
Beyond the curving sky?
No man has ever lived to tell
Just what it means to die.
Swift to life's terminal we trend;
(The sun seems short tonight)
God only knows what's at the end,
But I hope the lamps are white.

Part 5 Boxing Day Morning

So we slept throughout the night
Till morn, when Boomer's footsteps light
Before the sky at all was bright,
Awoke us from our dreaming.
Plodding round the common room
Footsteps like the crack of doom,
Then, very faintly through the gloom
We saw a "primus" gleaming.
With "Primus" stove and fire aglow,
Breakfast was soon on the go,
Then, just what happened, I don't know,
But Alex l gave a yell.
Startled by the sudden cry,
Wheeling on my heels did I
See that Alexander's eye
Had copped it good and well!
It seems that Joe had gotten tough,
And started playing rather rough,
So Ethel thought if she did cuff
Him smartly on the nose,
He might with better sense behave.
So feeling very, very brave,
A mighty smack to Joe she gave,
Where at that bright boy rose
And, without any more delay
Pushed her aside out of his way
Alas for poor old Alex J;
Her elbow was raised high.
'Twas then I heard poor Alex, yell,
As over, backwards, Ethel fell,
And with that elbow, sad to tell,
Banged Alex in the eye.

120

Breakfast now was ready
But I felt all queer inside,
And when I smelt John Pringle's steak
I really could have died.
The room was going round and round!
It would not stay at rest!
So I crawled back into my bunk
While the others ate with zest.

I once had a sweetheart but now I have none,
And since he has left me I live all alone;
I live all alone and contented I'll be,
For he loves another far better than me.

Chorus: - Green grow the laurel and soft falls the dew,
Sad was the day love; I parted with you;
I hope our next meeting will prove kind and true,
Don't change the green laurel for red, white and blue.

I wrote him a letter all crested in red;
He wrote me an answer, and guess what he said
"Keep your love letters and I will keep mine;
Write to your sweetheart and I'll write to mine."

Chorus: - Green grow the laurel and soft falls the dew,
Sad was the day love; I parted with you;
I hope our next meeting will prove kind and true,
Don't change the green laurel for red, white and blue

I wonder and wonder why women love men;
I wonder and never think how they love them,
For women are faithful and kind as you know
But men are deceivers wherever they go.

Chorus: - Green grow the laurel and soft falls the dew,
Sad was the day love; I parted with you;
I hope our next meeting will prove kind and true,
Don't change the green laurel for red, white and blue.

Green Grows the Laurel

I Have a Bonnet

I have a bonnet trimmed with blue.
Do you wear it? Yes I do.
I will wear it when I can
Going to the ball with my young man.

My young man has gone to sea,
When he comes back he'll play for me,
Tip to the heels and tip to the toes,
And that's the way the polky goes.

I have a bonnet trimmed with blue.
Do you wear it? Yes I do.
I will wear it when I can
Going to the ball with my young man.

Far away, on the edge of an African desert
Lay a young Irish soldier just breathing his last.
His comrades in battle, they all gathered round him
And sorrowfully list'd to his tale of the past.

He spoke of his home far away in old Ireland;
Of the grey haired old mother he left there in tears:
"If you live to go home, boys, tell her I died fighting,
Fought like a man with the brave fusiliers.

Just tell her I fought for the honour of Ireland;
Tell her I fought neath the red, white and blue;
Died, like a man, for my home and my country
And that's what a brave Irish soldier should do."

The Irish

They laid him to rest in the land of the stranger
Where the boom of the cannon disturbs not his sleep,
And his dear grey - haired mother far away in old Ireland
Thinks of her son who is so far o'er the deep.

Little she knows that her brave Irish hero,
Little she knows, as she lies there in tears,
That he'll never return to the land of his childhood
For they have laid him to rest with the brave Fusiliers.

Fusilier

Where The Grass Grows Green

I'm Denis Doyle from county Clare; I'm here at your command,
To sing a song in praise of home, our own dear native land.
I've sailed to foreign countries and to many climes I've been
But my heart is still in Erin where the grass grows green.
I love my native country and tho' richer lands I've seen
I can't forget old Ireland where the grass grows green.

Poor Paddy's often painted with a ragged coat and hat,
But his heart and hospitality's a lot to do with that.
Let slanderers say what they will, they cannot call him mean
For a stranger's always welcome where the grass grows green.
Let slanderers say what they will, they cannot call him mean
For a stranger's always welcome where the grass grows green.

It's true he has a weakness for a drop of something pure,
But that's a slight debility that many more endure.
He's fond of fun; he's witty - tho' his wit is not too keen
For there's tender hearts in Ireland where the grass grows green.
He's fond of fun; he's witty tho' his wit is not too keen
For there's tender hearts in Ireland where the grass grows green.

There's not a true born Irishman wherever he may be,
But loves the little emerald that sparkles in the sea.
May the sun of bright prosperity, shine peaceful and serene
And bring better days to Ireland where the grass grows green.
May the sun of bright prosperity, shine peaceful and serene
And bring better days to Ireland where the grass grows green

131

The sun, if sun there was that day,
(I can't remember, sad to say,)
Had reached it's Zenith in the sky
Ere from my bed again rose I,
To find that Molly, Beth, and Bill
(The Boomer bird) had had their fill
And now with Jake and Alexander,
Were planning, from the bay to wander,
And, by lonely path and cart track;
Over sand dunes, rocks and sea wrack,
O'er the cliffs, and o'er the hills,
Back again into Bushmills;
Thence, upon the King's Highway,
Return again to White park Bay.

But plans thus so securely laid
Are often turned about,
And though we'd settled thus and thus
Before our setting out;
Yet, ere Templastra has we reached
We changed our well–laid route,
For, though but few miles had we come,
We weary were, of foot.

Part 6 Boxing Day Afternoon

The current Youth Hostel at Whitepark Bay

A roadside shop a little shack
We then espied and entered in with glee.
Bill Boomer to the counter went:
"We want some lemonade to drink" quoth he.

Then we quaffed the fizzy liquid,
And we scoffed some hearty oatcakes
To give us druth enough to want to drink.
And they sure a thirst did give us
For they were as dry as ashes
And they weighed enough to make a cruiser
sink!

Then by weary ways and lonely
Did we come back to the hostel
As evening's shadows fell o'er land and sea.
Then huddled we together
In the ingle of the fire place
Till time it was for us to have our tea.

Over Here

Oh the praties they are small
Over here, over here,
Oh the praties they are small
And we dig them in the fall
And we eat them, coats and all
Full of fear.

Oh I wish we all were geese
Night and morn, night and morn,
Oh I wish we all were geese night and morn,
Oh I wish we all were geese night and morn,
For they live and die at peace
Till the day of their decease
Eating corn.

Oh we're down in the dust
Over here, over here,
Oh we're down in the dust
Over here
Oh we're down in the dust,
But that God in whom we trust
Will yet give us crumb for crust
Over here.

No help in hour of need
Over here, over here,
And God won't pay much heed
Over here.

Then whish't! Or He'll take the heed
And He'll rot the pratie seed
And send other mouths to feed
Over here.
I wish I was a duck
Over here, over here
To be eating clay and muck
Over here.

As I went out walking one fine summer morning
The birds in the bushes did warble and sing.
Gay laddies and lassies in couples were sporting,
Going down to the factory, their work to begin.

I spied one amongst them was fairer than any.
Her cheeks like the red rose that none could excel;
Her skin like the lily that grows in yon valley,
And she but a hard working factory girl.

I stepped up beside her, more closely to view her
But on me she cast such a look of disdain,
Saying, "Young man, have manners and do not come near me
For altho' I'm a poor girl, I think it no shame."

"Oh, it's not for to scorn you fair maid, I adore you
But grant me one favour, say, where do you dwell?"
"Kind sir, you'll excuse me, but now I must leave you,
For yonder's the sound of my factory bell."

"I have land I have houses adorned with Ivy;
I have gold in my pockets, and silver as well.
Sure if you'll come with me, a lady I'll make you,
And no more you need heed your factory bell."

The Factory Girl

"Now love and sensation rule many a nation.
Go marry a lady, and may you do well,
But I am an orphan, with ne'er a relation
And forbye, I'm a hard working factory girl."

With these words she turned, and with less she had left me,
And all for her sake I'll go wander away,
And in some deep valley where no one shall know me
I'll mourn for the sake of my factory girl.

A maid going to Cumber, her markets to learn,
To sell for her mammy three hanks of fine yarn.
She met with a young man along the highway
Which caused this young damsel to dally and stray.

"Oh sit ye beside me, I mean ye no harm;
Oh sit ye beside me this new tune to learn.
Here is three guineas your mammy to pay,
So lay by your yarn till the next market day."

They sat down together; the grass it was green,
And the day was the fairest that ever was seen.
"Oh the look in your eye beats a morning of May;
I could sit by your side till the next market day."

The maid she went home and the words that he said,
And the tune that he played her still rang in her head.
Said she, "I'll go seek him by land or by sea
Till he larns me the tune called "The next Market Day."

The Next Market Day

Come all ye strange amusers of high and low degree
And likewise pay attention and listen unto me.
I mean to leave this country bound for a land that's free
And bid farewell to all my friends, likewise to Innisfree.

When he rises in the morning he oils and combs his hair;
He dresses up in super fine and goes to meet his dear.
Her name I will not mention for it's offended she might be.
She's one of the finest flowers that bloom in Innisfree

When she rises in the morning she walks along the shore;
She watches for the big ship that bears her true love oer.
She watches the foaming billows as they roll upon the sea;
She sighs and cries "My Jimmy, you are far from Innisfree."

Innisfree

Farewell unto those bounding rocks that rise round Aranmore,
And likewise to you Mary, I will never see you more?
And when I am on the ocean no hills or dells to see,
I'll be thinking of you, Mary, so far from Innisfree.

You know I love you dearly - I could not love you more.
I love you better far than any man did before.
And if we chance to meet again, all in a land that's free
We will live and love each other as we did in Innisfree.

Lovely Mollie

Good-bye, lovely Mollie, I am now going to leave you;
To the East or West Indies I am now going to go.
Altho' we are parted, I'll be true and loyal hearted;
I'll be back, lovely Mollie, in the spring of the year.

I'll dress like a sailor, true love I'll go with you
Thro' the midst of all dangers I'll go without fear.
When the big ship is sailing and the wild waves are
raging
I'll be with you dearest Willie, to reel your topsail.

Your delicate hands, love, stout cables can't handle,
And your pretty little feet love, in the rigging can't
go.
Your delicate body wild waves can't endure, love;
Be advised, lovely Mollie, to the sea do not go.

The big ship set sail and left Mollie bewailing
Till her cheeks grew as pale as the lily that grows.
Her gay golden locks she kept constantly tearing
Saying, I'll sigh till I die love, will I e're see you
more?

Part 7
Boxing Day Evening

Amid the Dunes of lovely Whitepark Bay
Within the little white–washed hostel there,
We banked up the fire, lest closing day
Should leave us without light or heat, down where
The cold, dark, restless ocean stirred and groaned
And where the night wind, thru' the sea–grass moaned.

In silence sat we for what seemed an age,
Though scarcely more than half an hour at all.
The only sounds the turning of a page
In Pringle's book; the seabirds eerie call'
The wind; the crashingwaves upon the shore'
All building memories in each hearts' core.

The kettle boiled, unheeded, on the hearth.
No thoughts of food or drink were in our mind,
But only peace and calm, a dearth
Of which is in this would unkind.
And we were friends 'mid friends, so far
From even the slightest sights or sounds of war.

The Faery Song

How beautiful they are, the
Lordly Ones,
That dwell in the hills, in
the hollow hills.
They have faces like flower's
and their breath is a wind
That blows over summer
meadows,
White with dewy clover.

Their limbs are more white
than shafts of moonshine;
They are more fleet than the
March wind.
They laugh, and are glad,
and are terrible!
When their lances shake and
glisten
Every green leaf quivers.

How beautiful they are, the
Lordly Ones;
The Lordly Ones in the hollow
hills.

The Rocks

We have seen the gulls wheel
In circles of sight and sound
Above our heads;
We have felt the fingers of the grey wind
On our brows
We have heard the black skies thunder
About us;
We have felt the white lash of the seas
And the blue kiss of summer
                    On our cheeks.

The Dingle

I am a young jobber both foolish and airy,
The green hills of Kerry I came for to see;
I went back to Dingle to buy up some cattle
And I want you to listen to what happened to me.
As I entered the fair one Saturday morning
The first thing I saw was a long legged goat;
Bedad and says I for to commence our dealing
I think this bold hero is worth a pound note.

This daring old fellow I stood for to stare him,
Although I feared he was a monster to see;
He wore a long meggal as gray as a badger
That would reach from Dingle to Cahiaireer;
With a pair of long horns like any two bayonets
And just like two needles were pointed on top.
I am very sure you'd be a week laughing
If only he happened to hit you a rap.

I made my approach to the owner that held him,
A bargain we struck without much delay;
He said, "If you pay me down twenty two shillings
Some advice I will give you before going away.
This daring young hero was reared in the mountains;
In the year sixty–four he first used to drill;
And some of his comrades were hung and transported
And since he's determined some blood for to spill."

The old man departed and I was for starting:
Those words that he told me put me in despair.
The first jump he gave me, he near broke my left arm;
I jumped on his back and got hold of his hair.
Says I, "My bold hero, on your back I'm landed
And unless I will fall you may go where you will."
He ran thro' the streets like something distracted
And soon made his way towards Connor hill.

When he came near to Brandon I thought it was London;
I regretted my journey when I saw the sea.
He jumped into the water and swam right across it
Towards Castle Gregory to make a near way.
The waves of the ocean they put me in motion,
The fishes they ate all the nails from my toes,
And a mighty big mackerel jumped for my nostrils
And I thought he was gone with the half of my nose.

Puck Goat

When he came on the strand now quickly he ran towards
Clores or Castlemaine did he steer
To Milltown Killorglin and likewise Killarney.
And never cried stop till he came to Kenmare.
At length then he spoke "We have passed our head quarters
It's where our ancestors always have been;
Then let us return and take up our lodgings
At Curraghnamore where there's lots of poteen."

We done our returns and stopped there till morning,
It's during the night I sat up on his back;
As the day it was dawning he jumped from the corner
And towards Castleisland he went in a crack.
To the town of Tralee we next took our rambles
I think he was anxious to see some more sport.
Outside of the town we met some highlanders
He up with his horns and tore all their clothes

The highlander's shouted and bawled "Meela, murder!
Send for the polis and get him to jail!"
But the louder they shouted the faster my goat ran
And over the Basin he gave them leg bail.
On crossing the Basin I fell on the footway;
Away went the goat and I saw him no more.
Sure if he's in Ireland he's in Camp or in Brandon
Or away in the mountains somewhere remote;
But while I am living I've a story worth telling
Of my rambles thro' Kerry on the Dingle puck–goat!

The Gentle Maiden

There's one that is pure as an angel
And lovely as flowers in May,
And they call her the "gentle maiden"
Wherever she takes her way.
Her eyes have the glint of sunlight
As it brightens the blue sea - wave,
And more than the deep sea treasures
The love of her heart I crave.

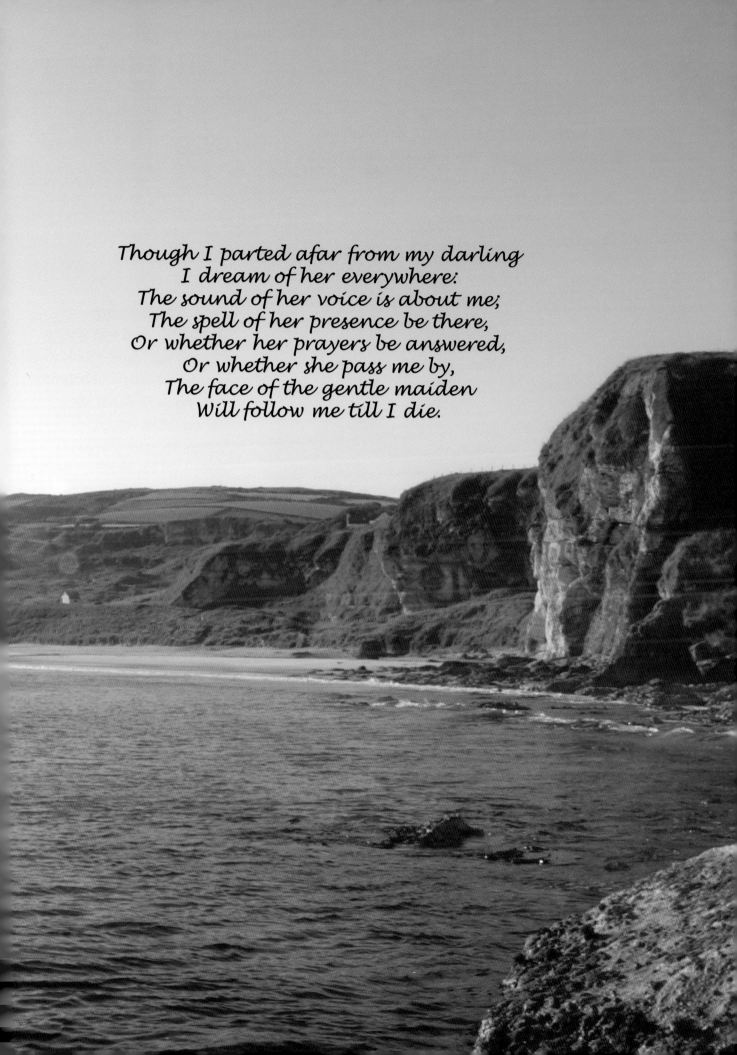

Though I parted afar from my darling
I dream of her everywhere:
The sound of her voice is about me;
The spell of her presence be there,
Or whether her prayers be answered,
Or whether she pass me by,
The face of the gentle maiden
Will follow me till I die.

Part 8 Wassailing at Whitepark

(Being the official report on the proceedings
of a small Section of Yhani; Christmas 1942).

Early one morning
Before the sun was rising
I heard the 'larm clock ringing
On the wooden floor below.
"Oh don't deceive me!
I'll not believe ye!
Surely its' not yet five o'clock
This cold December day?'

The winds that blew across the fields from Divis
Were tainted by the icebergs and the snow,
And I cried, "oh may the powers that be preserve us
For my legs are ten degrees below zero!"

With my rucksack o'er my shoulder
Sure there's no one could be colder
As I trammed it to the station ere the dawning.
And Macdonald I met there
He had brushed and combed his hair
And we hoped to reach Whitepark Bay in the morning.

There came smiling Alex Johnston when I looked I felt like death
There came Mollie looking jolly, by her side was bouncing Beth
But the sight, beneath the light that made me want to choke and cough,
Was that of William Boomer who just came to see us off!

Soon we said "Goodbye to Boomer, we must leave you
For our train, not much longer will delay,
But be brave, we'll have tea to receive you
When, (and if) you ever reach Whitepark Bay".

It's a long way to Portrush City;
It's a long way by train.
It's the wrong way; the more's the pity
If you don't change at Coleraine.
Goodbye, Ballymena;
Farewell Antrim town;
(It's a long way to end this ditty,
So pray I don't break down)

And when at last we arrived, not too late
(Turkey and bacon alive, alive–oh!)
We hoisted our rucksacks, (remember the
date)
And we forged ahead at a funereal rate
With our grub and our clothes;
Bannocks and loaves;

There's a long, long trail a winding
Into the town of Bushmills,
And my piston rods were grinding
Going up and down the hills.
When finally we got there
We had our noses tuned to tea;
But a Café found we nowhere
In sweet Bushmills by the sea

"Then cheer up my lads, tis of hiking I speak:
We've walked for three hours but we've still half a week,
So step out with a smile and we'll cover the mile
(I let out a groan for a blister did rile)
So let's cut out the fuss, and watch out for a bus:
We'll forwards while we can
And we'll die where we fall".
So down thro' the town we staggere`d all.

"Willie, I am growing weary,
Where, wherever can we be?
Speak to me some chatter cheery
Erc my soul ascendeth free".
"Yonder shineth Lisnagonouge,
Only three more miles to go".
"Mac, your words are like the honey——(ugh!)
Would someone please me tow?"

Ao yo ho! Ho yo ho! Walk my comrades, Ho yo ho!
Ho yo ho! Ho yo ho! Sing my comrades, Ho yo ho!
We will down the pathway go
Down the cart track let us flow;
Horizon goes dippy; the path is so slippy;
Hike my comrades, Ho yo ho!

"Now may I die, I sigh.
I feel that we may die at last.
What we did try is by –
Outside, the wind can blast!"
The shades of night had fallen fast
(Hark the wind! Hark the sea!)

"So come and raise your glasses high
To Whitepark by the sea.
There may be mice; the rooms like ice;
But we've our cups of tea.
And when at last the meal is done and we,
Ourselves have fed,
We light the fag or pass the bag
Weighed down with sweets like lead.

When thro' the doorway came at last
Ethel, Joe and William B.
Their plight was sad, twas plain to me
And soon we dished them out some tea.
"Gulp! Gulp! More tea please
 Ere we freeze round the knees!
"Gulp! Gulp! More tea. (Sneeze!)"
See them swill it down.

Good night, ladies;
Sleep tight, ladies;
Don't fight, ladies,
I want to get some sleep.
One lovely black eye!
(What if Alex should die?)
Only for saying that Ethel was
rough,
Oh! Look at that eye!
wind can blast!" the meal is done

You can't go to the Bushmills via cliff and rock,
For the gale your nose chills and your knee joints knock.
So we plodded to the highway over lots of muck,
We commandeered a shop and we tried our luck:
(I aint gonna drink ciderette no more!)

"Pringle, Pringle, show us some card tricks, do.
We're so sleepy and you've got nought else in view"
So I fingered the cards and I spread them;
I pattered and silently prayed then
But although hard I tried
And cussed till they fried
They still wouldn't say what I bid them.

In Whitepark Bay did Moll and Beth
A sumptuous breakfast - dinner fry,
That left us all with lack of breath
To ponder how one felt when death
Doth summon one to die.
So thrice three chairs (or almost so)
Were placed around the tasty foe.

Beloved porridge; homogenous mass;
(Beloved porridge shovelled in with milk);
And there was steak, and greasy bread first -
class
It all went down. Our skins they shone like silk
Praise the Lord and pass the ammunition;
Praise the Lord and push the blinkin' dish in!
Boomer has fulfilled his one ambition
And he can't get another bite down.

They are far from the bay
My comrades old?
Somewhere on this side of Dunluce
But the canned soups which they
Have left me to hold
Would fill a wheel barrow (packed loose)

Oh ye can take the high road
But I'll take the low road,
For the lower road would mortalise a fairy.
So they dandered slow along,
Joe and Bill and little John,
(Not forgetting Ethel clonks all the unwary)

On the ould narrow gauge, boys,
It's worth a fortnight's wage
(Ballymoney from the town of Ballycastle, oh!)
But the engine, it lost heart
Soon after we did start
So we were stranded on the line from Ballycastle, oh.

Oh comrades here, be of good cheer,
I tell you what we'll do;
The Yhani here are plentiful, the special's not in view.
We'll hold a ceillidhe here and now
Upon this bleak platform:"
You could hear the din, in Castlefinn, of Yhani keeping
warm.

Riding home, riding home,
Y.H.A's on its way, riding home.
Royal Billy crossed the Boyne,
But we trammed it to Ardoyne,
And at half twelve did I delve in my home.

Epilogue

The pale moon was rising
Above Divis mountain
The front door was locked and I had not my key.
By my boots badly hampered,
Thro' the window I clambered
And fell on my head, thence to bed with great glee.

It being in the month of May when fields were fresh and green,
I was forced to leave my native home, my age being scarce eighteen;
And when I parted with my dear her loving tears were seen;
In troubled mind I left behind my blue eyed mountain queen.

My father is a fisherman; he's on the raging sea;
My mother, she thro' seven long years sleeps cold beneath the clay.
My sisters and brothers four, I regard them with esteem
But little do ye know I weep full sore for my blue eyed mountain queen.

Farewell to Glenbeigh's lofty hills and to those mountains streams
Where sun or moon though in the gloom pours forth its brilliant gleams.
Her castle stands beneath the hill, bound round with laurels green;
But in America's plain I'll spend with my blue eyed mountain queen.

God speed the ship across the deep that steers my love to me;
The wind to fly her top sail wide, to waft her o'er the sea.
Her steel made bow has made a vow for to plough the waves with steam.
And in her breast to bear the crest of my blue eyed mountain queen.

My Blue

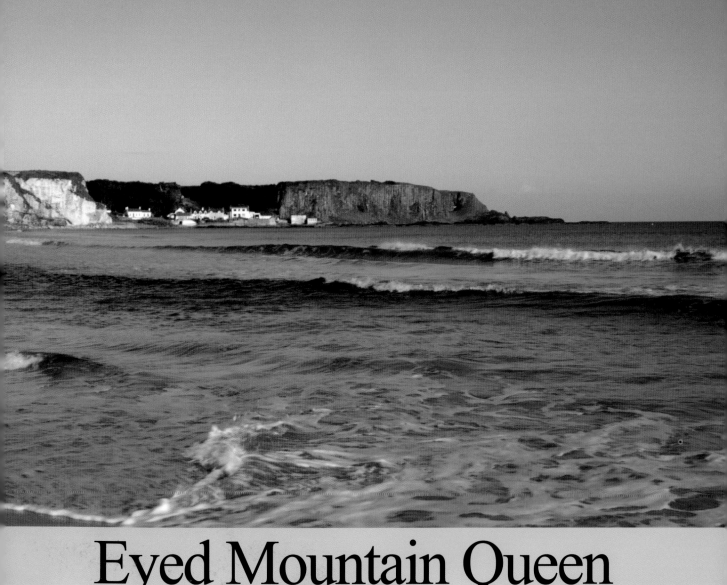

Eyed Mountain Queen